# EARTH & US
## CONTINUOUS

NATURE'S PAST & FUTURE

**ONE OF THREE BOOKS
CELEBRATING THE HUMAN CONNECTION WITH
NATURE'S FEATURES,
NATURE'S CREATURES,
AND NATURE'S PAST AND FUTURE**

BY J. PATRICK LEWIS • ILLUSTRATIONS BY CHRISTOPHER CANYON

DAWN PUBLICATIONS

## DEDICATIONS

For Mary and Tom — JPL

For Theresa and Steve with love and continuous friendship — CC

Copyright © 2001 J. Patrick Lewis
Illustrations copyright © 2001 Christopher Canyon

A Sharing Nature With Children Book

Library of Congress Cataloging-in-Publication Data

Lewis, J. Patrick.
Earth & us-continuous : earth's past and future / by J. Patrick Lewis ;
illustrated by Christopher Canyon.— 1st ed.
      p. cm. — (A Sharing nature with children book)
      ISBN 1-58469-023-2 (pbk.) — ISBN 1-58469-024-0 (hardback)
      1. Earth—Juvenile literature. [1. Earth.]    I. Title: Earth and
us-continuous. II. Canyon, Christopher. III. Title. IV. Series.
QB631.4 .L49 2000
550—dc21
                           2001002039

Dawn Publications
P.O. Box 2010
Nevada City, CA 95959
530-478-0111
nature@dawnpub.com

Published in Japan by Mikuni Publishing, Tokyo.
Printed in China

10 9 8 7 6 5 4 3 2 1
First Edition

Design and computer production by Andrea Miles

Ever since her birth
Ancient Mother Earth
Demonstrates her power
Spinning hour by hour.

Doesn't it seem strange?
Land and Sea arrange
Nature with the Sky—
We're just passers-by.

# EARTH

Longer ago than you could ever imagine, our
universe exploded outward. The Sun, one star
in an ocean of stars, formed about 5 billion
years ago. And 400 million years or so later, a
ball of molten rock called Earth took shape.
But thousands of centuries would pass before
our hot home, our blue balloon, cooled down . . .
for life.

The first worms wiggled,
Animals without backbones crept,
Plants began to paint the Earth.
The huge swamp forests followed after them.
Oh yes, and the dinosaurs rumbled for 150
  million years before they died out.

Late, very late in the world's calendar,
  we humans appear . . . .
But that is getting us far ahead of
  Earth's birth story.

One year is like a single drop of rain in the
  Earth's deep well of time.  Taste the rain.
  Don't let time drip away.

The Earth is a house, and its roof is the . . .

# SKY

For 300 miles up, until it thins into outer space, the Sky—our atmosphere—surrounds the Earth like a cocoon, protecting it from the Sun's harmful rays.

But it was not always so. Earth's rocks tell us tales about how the Sky and its climate have changed over time. Many chilly places today were once baking deserts, and hot tropical coral reefs once lined the now cold water coasts of Europe.

Insects were probably the first flyers—over 300 million years ago. Some dinosaurs also took to the air. And we humans in our flying machines are the last. Creatures of every species depend upon the careless ribbons of Sky that blow the breath of life.

Will our blue Sky cocoon always surround us? Only if we take care of that pale layer that protects the Earth.

The Sky is the dome to the bowl of the . . .

# SEA

Planet Earth might just as well be called Planet Water because there is so much of it. Over two-thirds of what surrounds us is Sea. And one great ocean—the Pacific—covers almost half the world.

In water we first evolved;
From water so much has come;
To water we owe our lives.
Water stands up and waves,
Roaring the Earth's applause.

Have you ever wondered what goes on down there under the Sea? Life! Life is going on . . . . and on . . . . and on. The Oceans hold the tallest mountain, the deepest trench, the greatest waterfall—and Sea animals without number, the likes of which you have never seen before.

Take a lesson from the Sea: Be strong and steady and full of life; be peaceful and calm. Be different.

To the web of the Sea flows a silken . . .

# RIVER

Who are the brother and sister of Rivers? Rain and snow!  Sometimes they spring from springs or from melting glaciers.  But ultimately all Rivers are born of the Sea.  Once on its way, a River seems to have a mind of its own, like a child, gurgling, tumbling, roughhousing.  When it reaches a Lake or the mouth of the Sea, a River slows down leaving rocks, sand and silt behind.  This sediment builds up in layers over time, very much like the layers of a sandwich.

Just think of all the amazing things a River can do!  You can swim in it, travel on it, fish in it, drink from it, wash in it, plant crops from it—or simply spend a lazy day watching it flow along.  With enough care, the Rivers will continue to amaze the children of our children's children.

A River is a shimmering reminder of change, second by second. Nothing but friendship remains the same.

The River is a path to the beauty of the . . .

# LAKE

What happens to an ice-cube tray when it's taken from the freezer? About 18,000 years ago, during the last Ice Age, thick, thundering and incredibly heavy masses of ice scooped out hollow places in the ground. When the climate warmed up over thousands of years, the ice melted and water filled the hollows to make Lakes . . . just like a melting ice-cube tray.

Most Lakes are fairly shallow and are fed by
   Rivers, but the oldest ones, like the Mountains,
   were formed when the crust of the Earth, broken
   into enormous continent-sized chunks, collided
   and crumpled.  Water rushed into the cracks to fill
   deep Lakes.

Earth is blessed with water in large and small cups,
   shining like bright coins. Save them for they are
   increasingly rare.

The Lake is the first step on the
                  stairway of the . . .

# MOUNTAIN

Mountains are Nature's pyramids.  But how did they get
  there in the first place?  Mother Earth built them
  herself—and it took millions of years.  Those enormous
  plates on the table of the Earth crashed into
  each other, buckling up the rocks like tin
  foil.  In fact, the plates are still crashing
  together but we don't notice it—
  at the rate of only a couple of
  centimeters every year—except,
  of course, for earthquakes!

But what rises high, sharp and
  craggy must do battle with
  wind, rain and ice that
  constantly knock off
  the sand and soil of
  Mountain tops and
  bear it away
  to Sea.

If you want visitors to know how special
the Earth is, first show them Mountains.

The Mountain is ice, and fire is a . . .

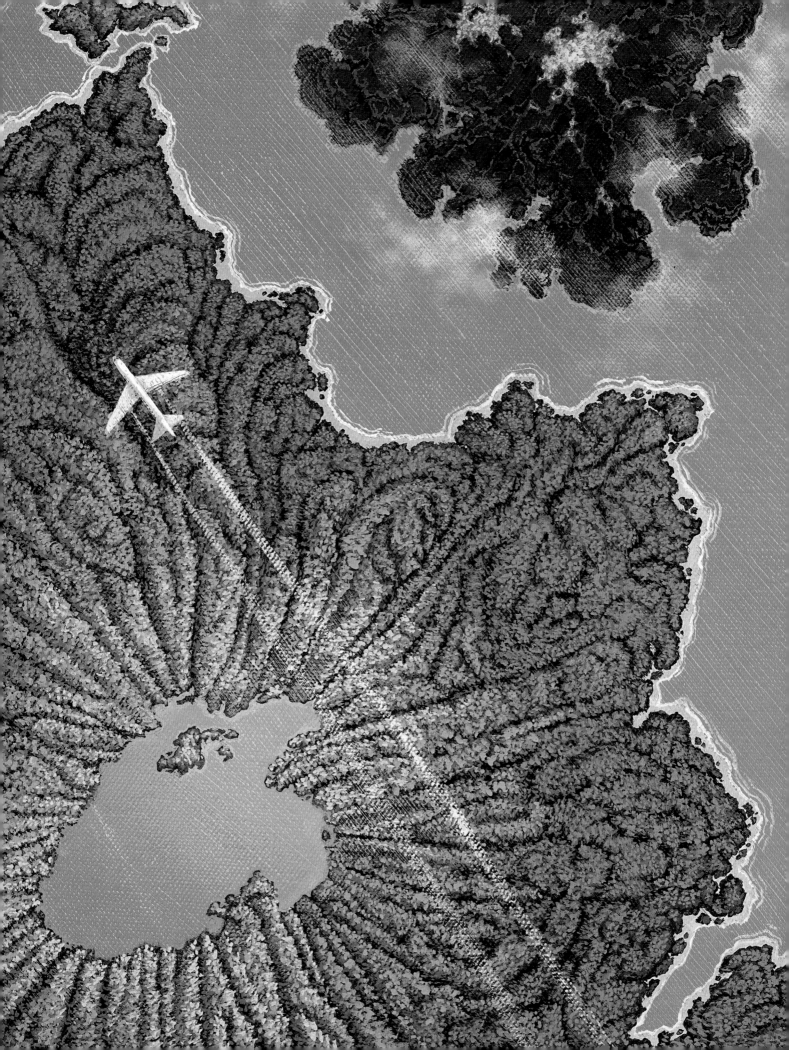

# VOLCANO

If you had a very good ear, you could rest it on the ground and hear the Earth's heart thumping!  But if the world's skin cracks, Earth from below destroys Earth above!  Lava— rock so hot that it melts—shoots through passages in the Earth's plates and streams down hillsides.  Clouds of ash fill the Sky, sometimes for days or weeks.

When Earth was just forming billions of years ago, its surface was probably covered with many active Volcanoes. Today, about 1500 of them blister the Earth, but only 50 or 60 are active.
Just as they destroy, Volcanoes also create new landscapes and habitats. Eventually, new life returns.

An exploding Volcano is sending you a message:  Live each day by starting a fire in the heart.

The Volcano is a mountain at war, and the valley of peace is the. . .

# WOODLAND

Every tree everywhere proudly raises its branches to the sun and moon. They have been doing so for millions of years. Where a flowering tree grows, so do the leaf-eating animals and those who live on leaf-eating animals. Which helps to explain why Woodlands have covered every continent.

Just think: Humans would never have evolved if it had not been for the forests. Why? Because this is where the apes—our closest living relatives—made their home.

But the Woodlands today face many enemies: cattle grazing, farming, logging, firewood-gathering—and acid rain, which gradually poisons trees.

Trees are keys that lock the House of Earth to the Sky. If the trees are lost, what will we do to replace them? They are also the keys to the future.

The Woodlands are nature's park, and nature's greenhouse is the . . .

# RAINFOREST

Who can count the millennia that have come and gone in
the making of the Rainforests?  As many as 200 kinds
of trees and thousands of animals may be found in a
single acre of tropical Rainforest.  Living far away
from this abundance, we might forget what natural
treasures we share.  But each year an area roughly
the size of Illinois or England is slashed, burned,
bulldozed, logged, destroyed, leaving wandering
scars of roads.

Humans have not been as kind to
Earth as Earth has been to humans.
About half of our original
rainforests are
already gone.

Imagine making homeless
millions of Earth's
inhabitants—
insects,
birds,
reptiles,
mammals.
We do it
every day
by destroying
more and more
Rainforest.

The Rainforest is renewal;
our ancient heritage is the. . .

# WETLANDS

Whether forest swamps or grassland marshes, the
Wetlands rose and fell with the rain—or lack of it.
Creatures grew and changed, lived and died, in these
gently flowing waters ages and ages before there was
ever a human being.

Wetlands bridge the past and the future. Much of what
lives here has not changed for millions of years. And
who can say what will become of these soggy bogs,
perfectly suited Wetland homes to alligators, turtles,
reptiles, storks and other birds.

Like much of our earthly wonders, Mother Nature's very
own birthplace—the Wetlands—are slowly being
destroyed by human hands intent on draining them.

If you want to discover the Museum of Life,
visit the Wetlands.

The Wetlands are rivers of grass
to the meadows of the . . .

# GRASSLAND

Once upon a time, long before humans arrived, Grasslands stretched endlessly across South Africa, Europe, Asia and the American Midwest. Here was a worldwide zoo park! Wild cattle, horses, camels, elephants, rhino, sheep, goats and deer were fair game for big cats, bears and wild dogs. But once humans began sweeping across the plains, many of the animals disappeared.

Amazingly, Grasslands can exist on so little water that they can "die" and yet come back to life with next season's rains. It's almost as if the Earth is showing us how vibrant it can be.

What makes prairies and savannas and pastures unique? In these fields, the spirit of the Earth walks with you.

The Grasslands are green gardens to the ivory fields of the . . .

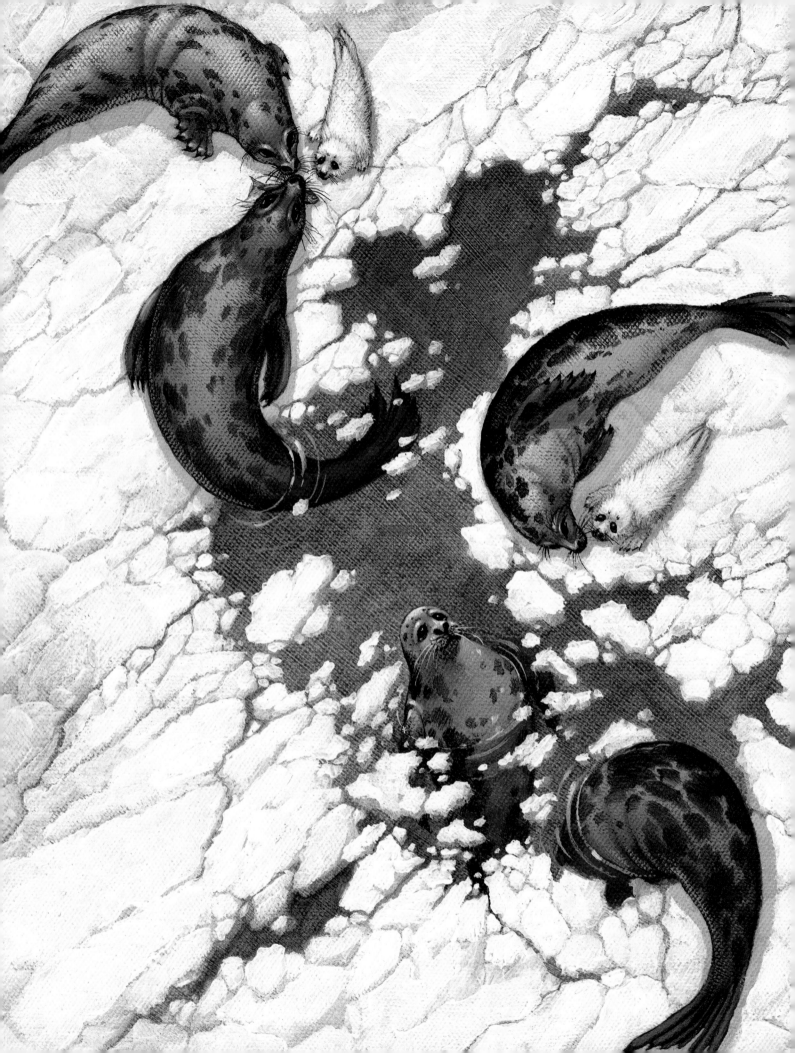

# ICE LAND

Cold deserts at both ends of Earth! Oh, how long ago did this beautiful blankness begin? Is this what the world would look like if the soup of living things never steamed and hissed and bubbled up into great forests, snakes and birds, fishes and mammals?

It would be comforting to know that now or a thousand years from now, you could live here, bundled up against the cold, and make friends with those who have found a way to live in what only seems to be a lifeless world. The Arctic fox, seals and snowbirds could show us the way in a land where ice is the floor and the windows and walls of life.

Whiteness everywhere you look! Admire the beauty, the stillness, the solitude. This is the last unspoiled frontier.

The Ice Land sets its face to the wind,
and so does the. . .

# HOT LAND

Rain, rain, come again! could be the song of the desert. But deserts do quite nicely without much rain. Long ago, one enormous continent—Pangaea, it was called—began to split apart. The Earth then was a very dry place indeed, especially the middle parts so far from water. It remains dry in many places because deserts cover nearly a third of the Earth's land.

Did you know that most deserts are rocky, not sandy?  Or that the world's deserts are spreading, because so many forests are being destroyed in bordering lands?

Here the wind is an artist drawing landscapes in the dunes.  There are no plants or trees standing in its way, so the wind whips along, carrying soil sometimes hundreds of miles.

Cactuses stand all day in the heat of the sun without complaining. Let your worries melt away . . .without complaining.

The Hot Land is a wide open door to a room called the . . .

# TOWN

People created Villages.
Villages became Towns.
Towns expanded into Cities.

But the spirit of them all is in the People who live and
  work and play there, who visit each other, make friends,
  and give thanks each day for the Community—

Which makes for Villages
 That become the Towns
 That grow into Cities.

Visit the Earth for wonders;
  visit a Continent for history;
  visit a Country for culture;
  visit a City for excitement;
  visit a Town for fun!

The Town is a book with a chapter called the . . .

# SCHOOL

The birth of a School is in the home.
The spirit of a School is in the student.
The wisdom of a School is in the teacher.
The heart of a School is in the knowledge.
The end of School . . . there is no end of School
  for there is so much to learn.

The time you spend in School
  is a time you will remember,
  for this is where you made
    friends with friends,
    made friends with books—
    and made time for both.

The School is a flower in the house of the . . .

# EARTH

Ever since her birth
Ancient Mother Earth
Demonstrates her power
Spinning hour by hour.

Doesn't it seem strange?
Land and Sea arrange
Nature with the Sky—
We're just passers-by.

For 30 years J. Patrick Lewis was a college professor, teaching economics. Now he plays with words and hangs out with kids at elementary schools. He is out to prove that "poetry is ear candy," and to inspire a simpatico connection with the natural wonders that surround us. "If there is a better way to spend a lifetime," he says, "I can't imagine what it would be." This is his second book with Dawn Publications.

Christopher Canyon is irrepressibly playful as well as passionate about illustrating children's picture books. He teaches illustration at the Columbus College of Art & Design in Columbus, Ohio, is a frequent speaker at professional events, and his illustrations have been displayed in several national exhibitions. But his favorite audience is children and he makes a point of visiting schools often. Two of his previous books for Dawn Publications, **The Tree in the Ancient Forest** and **Stickeen: John Muir and the Brave Little Dog**, won the Benjamin Franklin Award as best illustrated children's books of the year.

# THE EARTH TRILOGY

BY J. PATRICK LEWIS, ILLUSTRATED BY CHRISTOPHER CANYON

Earth & You—A Closer View: Nature's Features
Earth & Us—Continuous: Earth's Past and Future
Earth & Me—A Family Tree: Nature's Creatures (available Spring, 2002)

## OTHER BOOKS ILLUSTRATED BY CHRISTOPHER CANYON

*The Tree in the Ancient Forest*, by Carol Reed-Jones. The plants and animals around a grand old fir are remarkably and wonderfully dependent upon each other. Christopher's magical realism, and Carol's cumulative verse serve both to inform the mind and inspire the soul.

*Stickeen: John Muir and the Brave Little Dog* by John Muir as retold by Donnell Rubay. In this classic true story, the relationship between the great naturalist and a small dog is changed forever by their adventure on a glacier in Alaska.

*Wonderful Nature, Wonderful You*, by Karin Ireland, shows how nature is a great teacher, reminding us to bloom where we are planted. This popular book celebrates nature's diversity and strong character traits—and with a light touch, suggests how humans can follow nature's example and make good choices.

## A SAMPLING OF NATURE AWARENESS BOOKS FROM DAWN PUBLICATIONS

*Birds in Your Backyard* by Barbara Herkert, is an excellent tool to help kindle the spark of interest in birds at an early age, and so establish a life-long passion for nature in general, and birds in particular.

*Under One Rock: Bugs, Slugs and other Ughs* by Anthony Fredericks. No child will be able to resist looking under a rock after reading this rhythmic, engaging story—the perfect balance of fact, fiction, and fun.

*Do Animals Have Feelings, Too?*, by David Rice presents fascinating true stories of animal behavior, and then asks the reader whether they think the animal is acting on the basis of feelings or just instinctively.

*Animal Acrostics*, by David M. Hummon. Acrostic poems are a wonderful way to encourage children to write creatively. These "vertical poems" are amusing, clever, and informative.

*Salamander Rain, A Lake and Pond Journal* by Kristin Joy Pratt-Serafini. This young author-illustrator's fourth book is a "planet scout's" pond and lake journal—a subject known to be wet and muddy, but fun! Kristin is the teenage "eco-star" made famous by her books *A Walk in the Rainforest, A Swim through the Sea,* and *A Fly in the Sky.*

Dawn Publications is dedicated to inspiring in children a deeper understanding and appreciation for all life on Earth. To order, or for a copy of our catalog, please call 800-545-7475. Please also visit our web site at www.dawnpub.com.